DANCE TEAM

Mary Kaye Coachman

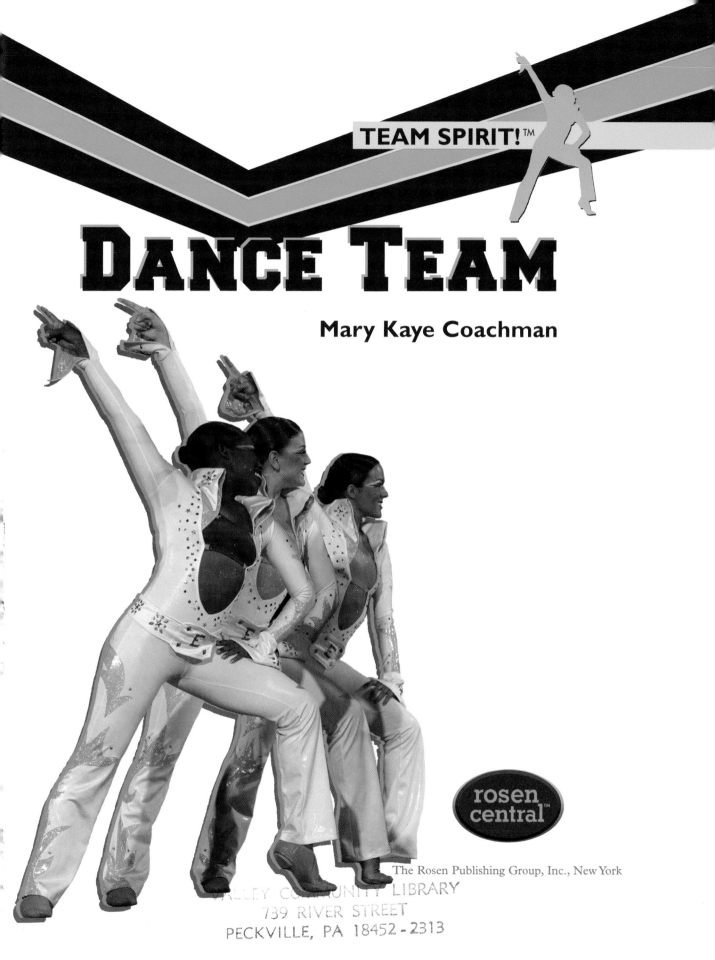

rosen central™

The Rosen Publishing Group, Inc., New York

I would like to dedicate this book to my mother, Dr. Amelia Rose Sykes Steelman, who gave up countless hours, days, weeks, months, and years driving me to dance lessons at the Betty Hogue School of Dance Arts in Greenville, Texas. I realize now that she sacrificed both her time and a great deal of money in order for me to participate in an activity that meant so much to me and ultimately led to my career. I am grateful to her every day of my life for leading me to this profession.

Published in 2007 by The Rosen Publishing Group, Inc.
29 East 21st Street, New York, NY 10010

First Edition

Library of Congress Cataloging-in-Publication Data

Coachman, Mary Kaye.
Dance team/Mary Kaye Coachman.—1st ed.
    p. cm.—(Team spirit!)
Includes bibliographical references and index.
ISBN 1-4042-0731-7 (library binding)
1. Marching drills—Juvenile literature 2. Dance—Juvenile literature.
I. Title. II. Series: Team spirit! (New York, N.Y.) III. Series.
GV1797.C77 2007
791—dc22
                                                                    2005037505

Manufactured in the United States of America

On the cover: The Rowlett High School Silver Rhythm Dancers of Dallas, Texas, perform at a football game in Mesquite, Texas, in November 2005.

CONTENTS

THE SPIRIT KICKERS

As the football players make their way to the locker room at the end of the second quarter of the big game, other groups of athletes are preparing to take the field for their chance to shine and entertain the crowd. They include the members of the marching band with their polished instruments, the color guard carrying their brightly colored flags, the majorettes with their shiny batons, and the dance team in their flashy costumes. They stand at attention on the sidelines in anticipation of the fun and excitement of putting on the long-awaited halftime show.

Sitting in the audience are many young children with dreams of strutting their stuff on that same football

Although dance teams are most visible to the public during the football and basketball seasons, there is much more to the dance team world than halftime shows. The dancers have their own competition season, during which the shows and costuming are more elaborate.

field. Some will be on the sports team, some will be in the band, some will twirl a baton or toss a flag, and of course, some will earn a coveted spot on the dance team. The students in the spotlight on the field tonight once sat in the same stands and dreamed the same dreams. For the young people dreaming of being on the dance team, it is not too soon to begin the preparations to make their dreams come true.

Heather Chapman waited ten years before she had her chance to audition for the Ellison High School Emeralds, who cheer for the school's football team, the Eagles. She had watched the dance team with joyful anticipation every Friday night since she was three years old. When Friday came, she put on her green and white uniform, which looked just like those worn by the high school girls she admired, and off she went to cheer on the football team, while watching every move of the Emeralds. Heather loved those games, but it was really the half-time show that she came to see. When the drum major blew the forward march whistle, Heather stood up in her seat so she would not miss a step made by her idols on the field. Her favorite part of the dance team's presentation was always the high kick line. As the team hooked up, arm over arm, Heather knew the precision kicks would be next. Every kick seemed perfect to her, and she knew someday she would kick like that, too.

Dance teams, such as the Emeralds, have pushed beyond their tra-ditional roles as halftime entertainment at football games or as part of the spirit team that boosts school pride at pep rallies. The dance team

As these seven young ladies strike a pose on the sideline, it does not seem so long ago that they sat in the bleachers admiring the dance team girls in those same uniforms, dreaming of the day when they might each get to wear one.

activity is now a sport in its own right, complete with a full set of local, regional, and national championships. Through innovation, dance team has become an American icon that has earned its unique spot among the pageantry arts.

CHAPTER 1

Dance Team History

Dance teams can be so exciting to watch that some fans go to football games just for the halftime entertainment. In fact, it was the search for something to make halftimes more entertaining that brought about the creation of the most well-known dance team in existence today. In 1939, Dr. B. E. Masters, the dean of Kilgore College, hired Gussie Nell Davis to find a way to put enough spark in the halftime

The captain of the world-famous Kilgore College Rangerettes, adorned in the trademark red, white, and blue uniform, leads her team in a parade performance.

shows to keep fans in their seats and bring more women to the college. Davis had already taken her pep squad at Greenville High School in Greenville, Texas, to new heights when she added rhythm and dance steps to its marching drills. She took this idea a step further at Kilgore when she decided the answer to Dean Masters's request was having a precision dance team perform with the band at halftime. On September 12, 1940, the world-famous Kilgore College Rangerettes made their debut, beginning a sport that would change halftime shows everywhere.

With the popularity of the Rangerettes, precision dance teams began appearing at high schools and colleges all across the United States. Young

Gussie Nell Davis is a legend in the world of dance and drill team. It is because of her vision and creation of the Kilgore College Rangerettes that the popularity of this halftime entertainment industry has grown to such enormous proportions.

girls wanted to attend football games with their parents just so they could watch their idols perform their precision high kick routines at halftime. Girls everywhere aspired to grow up and wear colorful short skirts with white hats and white boots, hooking up in a line with their teammates to perform high kicks that would bring booming applause from an audience. For many young ladies, the dream did not end when they made their high school dance team; instead, that experience only left them wanting more.

Angela Mather was one of those young dancers whose success on her high school team led to an even bigger dream. She was determined that one day she would wear the famous red, white, and blue uniform of the Kilgore College Rangerettes.

She would do whatever it took to earn a spot on Davis's legendary dance team. With that goal in mind, Angela worked out and practiced

From a page out of history, this Rangerette line shines with the pride that is still a symbol of dance team members today as they take the field in their uniforms. Although the skirt length has become much shorter over the years, the smiles on the dancers remain timeless.

all summer. She even attended the Rangerette Summer Camp in hopes of learning the trademark style of the world-famous group. Finally, the day came for her to pack her suitcase and head out for the small east Texas town. No one could have prepared her for what was in store for her once she arrived on the campus of Kilgore College. The Rangerette hopefuls were put through hours of rigorous training for approximately a week and a half before their final audition. Though many of them, tired and exhausted, wanted to go home, Angela continued to work hard and push herself toward her dream. Successful, Angela spent the next two years kicking with her Rangerette teammates in the red, white, and blue.

Parents shared the dreams with their daughters and wanted to see them on the football field someday. Soon, dance studios saw an increased interest in dance as more parents sought ways to help their daughters prepare for the intense tryouts that they were sure to face. Girls took dance lessons for years, trying to acquire the skills needed for their high school dance team auditions. Eventually, parents and students began to ask, "Why wait until high school?" With the interest growing and training beginning earlier and earlier, dance teams began popping up for younger girls. Many junior high schools, middle schools, intermediate schools, and even elementary schools began organizing teams of their own.

In 1972, the dance team concept grew beyond the public school and college football venues with the creation of the Dallas Cowboys Cheerleaders, the first National Football League (NFL) cheerleading squad. Tex Schramm, general manager of the Dallas Cowboys at the time, saw the need for more entertainment on the sidelines since NFL football had become more than just a sport. Schramm and Dee Brock, who managed the high school students who had been cheering for the Cowboys, discussed the need for a new look. Eventually, they hired Texie Waterman, a Dallas dance studio owner, to take the traditional sideline format of cheerleaders and create a group of attractive and accomplished dancers to perform during the game.

In their white shorts, blue shirts, and white boots, the Dallas Cowboys Cheerleaders made their debut to kick off the 1972–1973 NFL season,

Profile of an NFL Dancer/Cheerleader: Mary Frances

Mary Frances Coachman was a young dancer who knew at an early age that she wanted to be an NFL cheerleader and dance on the sidelines at professional football games. She had an unforgettable experience in middle school when Miss Ashley Elmore, her dance studio instructor, entered her students in the Dallas Cowboys Cheerleaders' dance contest. They were quite successful, earning the opportunity to dance at halftime during a Dallas Cowboys' game.

The students would never forget the excitement of sharing the field with the beautiful Dallas Cowboys Cheerleaders. That was only the beginning of the dream building for Mary Frances. She spent the next few months watching her teacher prepare for the Dallas Cowboys Cheerleader auditions herself. Imagine her excitement when she heard the news . . . Miss Ashley was a Dallas Cowboys Cheerleader! It was then that she knew in her heart that someday she would have just such an experience.

While in college, Mary Frances began going to the Houston Texans football games, where she immediately noticed the talented girls dancing on the sidelines. She loved the red boots worn by the Houston Texans Cheerleaders. Encouraged by the director for the Texas Aggie Dance Team, her roommates, and her own young dance students, she auditioned. Mary Frances's childhood dream came true; she was now an NFL cheerleader.

The Dallas Cowboys Cheerleaders entertain crowds with their classic style and jazzy performances. Thousands of dancers travel to Dallas each year in April to audition for a spot on this NFL cheerleading squad, which has earned the title America's Sweethearts.

bringing jazz dance to the pro football sidelines. Their popularity grew as they began making appearances on television shows, in movies, and overseas, and the team soon became known as America's Sweethearts. The trend spread throughout the NFL as other teams created their own sideline dance squads. Soon, it seemed that every professional football team had its own group of glamorous young ladies dancing on the sidelines, delighting fans of all ages. The dreams of young girls followed this progression as they hoped to continue dancing after college at this professional level.

Football is no longer the only sport whose sidelines are enhanced by dancers. Basketball courts nationwide have become stages for dance teams as well. Just as the Dallas Cowboys and the Houston Texans have cheerleaders, the Dallas Mavericks have the Maverick Dancers and the

Houston Rocket fans are entertained by the Power Dancers. Paula Abdul was a Los Angeles Lakers Girl before she became a famous entertainer. So what was once an activity for high school and college students has become a favorite pastime for young girls and women of many ages, as well as for high school boys. Not only can girls dance on teams as early as preschool age, they can also continue through college and even after college at the professional level. Whether watching high school or college halftime shows or admiring the glamorous NFL cheerleaders dancing on the sidelines, young women are building dreams and goals as they aspire to be those performers themselves.

Since Gussie Nell Davis created the Rangerettes in 1940, the performance venues for dance teams have expanded far beyond the football field. As dance team became more popular, teams and organizations created competition circuits across the country to recognize the most accomplished units. While dance teams still perform at sporting events, the network of dance team championships has grown to the point that teams may compete every weekend, January through March. Dance teams are no longer dependent on sports teams for performance opportunities. In fact, the halftime shows have become warm-up sessions for a dance team's competitive season.

The rise in popularity of these competitions has contributed to many changes in the dance team world. The drive to outshine the competition has led to flashy costuming, elaborate backdrops, more intricate choreography, more intensive training, and even the addition of male dancers to add to the creativity and variety of the routines.

CHAPTER 2

Making the Team

To young people everywhere who have dreamed of being on a dance team, the spring, usually March or April, brings the long-awaited dance team audition. Some schools hold an additional fall audition, but the main focus is on the spring audition. The audition process begins with the paperwork. The application packet may be lengthy, but it is informative. It includes the rules, polices, procedures,

It is never too early to begin preparations for dance team auditions. Students often begin taking dance classes even before they are in elementary school. These dance lessons can help build the confidence and poise needed to succeed in the tryout process.

financial obligations, and rehearsal schedule for the team.

It is very important to read this material before making the commitment to try out. Being a dance team member is not just about the performance and the glamour. It is a big responsibility, and members must be willing to make sacrifices and meet all of the requirements of the team. The application must be signed by the student and a parent or guardian and turned in to the director of the team. It is important to meet all deadlines to set a good impression from the beginning of the process. Late, incomplete, or messy paperwork indicates a lack of responsibility and may hinder one's chances of making the team.

In addition to the application, most teams require teacher recommendations and extensive grade verifications. It is not enough to be a talented dancer. A good dance team member must have the "total package." Making good grades, having the respect of teachers, and setting a good example for others are all important qualities for dance team members. These are areas that must be thought about and worked on long before the audition date. A dance team director will not want to jeopardize the integrity of his or her program by taking on a member who may become a potential discipline problem or who will not be able to keep her grades up.

Many schools have academic and behavior requirements for students who participate in extracurricular activities. Students who represent the school may be held to a higher standard than other students. If a student has difficulty with her studies already, she may find it hard to balance her schoolwork with the extra demands of dance team rehearsals and performances. Therefore, time management is an important part of the preparation for the audition.

The Tryout

Once the paperwork process is complete, the most exciting part of the audition begins. Finally, the potential members get to do what they love most—dance! Each team has its own style and technique of dance that the applicants must learn during several days of instruction prior to the judging day. Some teams may teach one routine for tryouts, while others teach two or three different combinations to introduce each style of

As an instructor demonstrates the correct form necessary for a turn, the candidates watch with intensity to grasp every important detail of her technique and style. This attention to detail is an important part of a dance team audition.

dance the new members will be expected to perform. The dance steps may be taught by the director of the team or the officers, and often the returning team members may be able to help the hopefuls learn the styles and techniques that will be expected of them as they audition.

Some of the applicants will pick up the choreography with little difficulty, but most will find that they must practice hard when they go home at the end of each day. The tryout material may be challenging for the less experienced dancers, and unfortunately, it is not uncommon for a few students to drop out before the audition day. Sometimes students make the mistake of underestimating themselves, giving up on their dreams prematurely. It is important for each applicant to finish the audition process and let the judges make the decision.

The final step in the audition process is sometimes the most frightening. The paperwork has been checked, the grades have been verified, the teacher recommendations have been reviewed, the dances have been learned, and now the judging must begin. Often, each candidate will be interviewed by the judges prior to dancing. The candidates must be prepared to explain why they want to be on the team, what they can offer to the team, and what they have done to prepare for the tryout.

After the interview, the candidates must perform for the panel of judges. Most teams do not require the candidates to dance individually but in small groups of three to six students at a time. The judges are trained to look for potential in the candidates. Technique and style are important, and showmanship is a huge plus. The judges will be looking for boys and girls who can radiate energy. A dancer's love for performing must be obvious. Each candidate must have confidence in himself or herself. If one candidate in the group forgets a step or makes a mistake, the others must be able to continue dancing, showing the judges that they know their stuff.

Every student has been interviewed and performed the routines. The judging is over and the waiting begins! Not every team announces its results in the same way. Some teams post a list shortly after the judges have completed their scores. This list will include the names or audition numbers of the new team members. Some teams have all of the candidates return to the gym to hear the new members' names or numbers called out. Another popular method is to give each candidate a sealed envelope with a letter of congratulations for those

Before learning the audition routines, the candidates are guided through a series of warm-up and stretching exercises to prepare their bodies for the demands of the rigorous dance team tryout. Being in top physical condition is just as important as having the correct dance technique and style.

who make the team or a note of encouragement for those who do not. No matter what the result, each student will have grown as a person and learned something valuable in the process.

Marilyn Santiago could not remember a time when she had not thought about being on her high school dance team. She so vividly remembered the first football game she went to with her family. Marilyn was in awe of the shiny uniforms with their sequins and fringe trim as the dance team strutted onto the field. But her favorite parts were the white boots and hats

Enrolling in a dance studio can provide a valuable experience for young students who hope to dance on a high school, college, or even professional team someday. Many studios have their own competitive dance teams.

worn by the dancers. As she watched the girls dance with such pride, she turned to her sister and said, "I want to be one of those girls, too!"

The spring of her eighth-grade year finally arrived, and Marilyn picked up her tryout packet. She attended every rehearsal and practiced for hours on end at home. She was so anxious for tryouts to end so she could begin practicing with the rest of the team. The director handed each candidate her envelope at the end of the final day. Marilyn was not prepared for what she read. She read it again, through

tear-filled eyes. How could this be? Her best friend made it. Surely this was a mistake. But no, it was not. She did not make the team. Suddenly she felt bitter toward the team she had admired since childhood.

For the next few days, Marilyn's sister comforted her and convinced her that it was not the end of the world. Marilyn did go to the games in the fall, for she wanted to watch her friends who had made the team. She enrolled in a dance class at a local studio. When it was time for spring auditions again, her wounds had healed. With more determination than ever, she went through the whole process again. Her friends who made the team before helped her every day. When the envelope was placed in her hand, she felt the butterflies in her stomach. She slowly opened it, and again, she had to read it twice. Through tear-filled eyes, she read, "Congratulations, new dance team member!"

Preparing to Perform

Once the new team members have been selected, it is time for orientation, uniform fitting, ordering supplies, and learning the ropes. The director will schedule spring meetings to meet the new members and their parents. Summer rehearsals and camp will be scheduled to make sure that the team is ready for the first halftime performance. It is important for the entire family to be familiar with the practice calendar, making sure that summer trips and vacations do not conflict with the dance team commitment. Just as the football players have practice before the school term resumes, so do the dance team members. There are dance skills to be mastered and choreography to be learned for the upcoming halftime shows.

A big part of these summer preparations is dance team camp. Some teams go away to a camp held on a college campus or in a hotel. These "resident" camps involve taking classes with girls from other schools and usually include evaluations and competitions. Other teams hold a private camp at their own school, but they can still enjoy daily evaluations. There are many different dance companies that offer both types of camp curriculum. During camp, the team members may learn several different routines for their upcoming performances. There may be a "show-off" day that friends and family can attend to watch the teams perform the routines they have learned during the week. This is a great time for the new members to begin getting accustomed to performing in front of an audience. Before stepping onto the football field for their first halftime show, they will perform for their families and friends.

Following camp, there will be more days of summer practice. During this time, more routines may be learned, and those learned at camp will be fine-tuned. The girls must learn to make every movement look uniform. Time will be spent learning to stretch properly to acquire the flexibility necessary for kicks, splits, leaps, and other extensions required of the team members. In addition to working on the dances, technique classes may be held to improve the skills of every dancer.

Practice doesn't stop when school starts. Some teams hold rehearsals early in the morning before the school day begins. Others rehearse after school when other students have gone home for the day. This is all

Summer dance camps provide a great opportunity for dance team members to bond with their own teammates and meet students from other schools while taking classes from expert instructors on a college campus.

part of the commitment a dance team member must be willing to make. For many schools, the dance team also meets during a class period, and the members receive class credit in fine arts or physical education.

For a team to keep up with all of these rigorous activities, every dancer must be in top condition. This requires proper conditioning, nutrition, and rest. It is important to begin rehearsals with a short aerobic session to warm the muscles, followed by a stretching session to attain maximum flexibility and, finally, strengthening exercises to improve endurance. Dancers must also keep their bodies hydrated before, during, and after rehearsal. Healthy eating habits will benefit every dancer, and many directors spend time educating the team about the importance of proper nutrition. In the art of dance, the dancer's body is his or her instrument, and care must be taken to keep that instrument fine-tuned.

CHAPTER 3

Elements of Dance Team

A team can be defined as a group of people working on a common task or engaged in an activity together. For a dance team to be successful, teamwork is crucial. A good team must have a group of talented dancers, but these dancers must be able to work well together toward a common style.

Being a good dancer is not enough to be a good dance team member. Each student must adapt to the style of the

As team members work hard to prepare for contest season, more experienced dancers may be challenged even further by entering solo competitions. While team dances require uniformity of movement and style, solo performances give the advanced dancer an opportunity to showcase her individuality.

team and be willing to work well with the director and the other team members. Dance team is not about individual dancing; it is about talented individuals dancing together as one unit.

Sometimes it may be necessary for a dancer to conform to the style and technique level of the majority of the group. The director or coach will set the standard and guide the members to work to meet or exceed that standard. The weaker, less experienced dancers will have to work hard to improve their technique, while the stronger, more experienced dancers will have to work to adjust to the style and level of difficulty established for the team. Teamwork plays a big role here, as the team members work to help each other. Every dancer must make a commitment to contribute to the unity of the team. The team has to become more important than the individual.

Organization of the Squad

Beginning at the top, the person in charge of the entire group is, of course, the director. He or she has the final say in everything that happens and every decision that must be made. Many teams also have an assistant director to share in the responsibilities. The directors are responsible for the selection of music, costuming, choreographing dances or selecting choreographers, teaching routines, making and enforcing the rules, arranging performances, and working with the students and parents to see that the team is successful.

While some girls dream of being a dance team member, others dream of leading their dance team as an officer, possibly even top officer someday. Their reasons may be different, but they know they will not be happy until they have accomplished that goal.

The officers for some teams wear a different color uniform than do the other team members, and they dance in front of the line. The officers at Kilgore College are easily recognized. There are five Rangerettes in white uniforms dancing in front of the other talented young ladies in the red, white, and blue uniforms. At some schools, the officers' hats are different colors, with each rank having its own unique

Practice can become tiresome while working on a difficult routine. It can be beneficial to stop occasionally and have a team-building activity. A director or social officer can reenergize the team with a game or other fun exercise to release tension and lighten the mood of a strenuous rehearsal.

color. During the halftime show, the names of the officers may be announced, giving those members extra recognition. However, most of the young women who lead their teams would do so without any of this extra flair or attention. True leaders thrive on guiding, helping, and preparing their teammates for the job at hand.

The officers of the team will work under the supervision of the directors, but they must never attempt to take on the role of director. The

The Selection of Officers

Typically, dance team officers are selected in tryouts, which are usually held after the team auditions. A thorough officer tryout includes a personal interview with the judges, performing a group and/or solo routine, and sometimes choreographing an original dance combination or routine. Often, officer candidates must put together a notebook or portfolio showcasing their accomplishments and strengths. In addition to being talented dancers, it is important for the officers to exhibit strong leadership skills. For some schools, the decision is based entirely on judges' scores, while others include the vote of team members and the director.

While qualifications vary from group to group, there are a number of traits that good officers possess. These include self-respect and respect for the team and the director, determination, a willingness to help other team members, self-discipline, patience, fairness, and the ability to lead by example. A good officer must also be responsible and prepared.

number of officers for each team may be determined by the number of team members. However, some teams have a traditional number of officers with set ranks. The Emeralds, for example, always have a top officer, the colonel, and a captain, who is second in command. The

For some teams, the officer uniform is different from the team uniform, making it easy to spot the officers during a performance. While an officer's uniform may be white, her hat may be a different color as an indication of her rank.

team will have two or three lieutenants each year, depending on the size of the team. Some teams have unranked officers. The officers of a team may help with choreography, teaching and polishing routines, and helping team members. In addition to the dance officers, social officers exist on some teams. Their job may be to motivate the team with team-building activities. These activities are especially helpful at the beginning of the year to help the new members get to know each other better or to break the stress during the hectic times.

One favorite activity is to have the team members talk about the team while sitting in a circle. Usually, one team member is given a small stuffed animal and is called upon to say something positive about the team. The stuffed animal is then thrown to another team member, who will do the same thing. The animal will be thrown from person to person until each team member has had an opportunity to speak. The key to using any team-building activity successfully is to make sure everyone participates, while keeping the activity short.

CHAPTER
4

Performance Opportunities

Dance team is a year-round activity. A favorite phrase among both directors and students is, "There is no off-season in dance team." Dance team goes from season to season, filling the entire school year. For most teams, the seasons are football season, basketball season, competition season, and spring show season. The spring show is a big recital at the end of the year. It is usually held in

The annual spring show can be an exciting performance venue, offering unique costuming and creative choreography. The dance numbers included in the show may present the entire team or showcase specialty groups or soloists.

the auditorium or gym of the school. For many teams, this is the big fund-raiser of the year.

Football season may be the primary focus of many teams. Football games usually begin in August, with the regular season ending in November. However, for those schools fortunate enough to have a strong football team, the playoffs can run into December. Basketball games begin in October or November, with the playoffs running sometimes until March. The major dance team competitions begin in January, with most dance team companies holding their national contests at the end of March or early April. April and May are the main spring show months, and of course, tryouts for the next year are usually held in April. (For most teams, everyone, including current members, tries out each year.) Summer practices are held in June, July, and August. Not only is there no off-season, but these seasons overlap, keeping dance team busy year-round.

Dance team members love to dance and perform every chance they get. However, most seem to have a favorite season for one reason or another. For many dancers, the best season of the year is football season. These dancers delight in cheering for their school's team on the sidelines and then taking the field to strut their stuff during the halftime show. They enjoy performing under the bright stadium lights in front of a huge crowd in the stands, as well as in front of the dance team of the opposing school.

Other dancers prefer basketball season. They love to hear the roar of the basketball crowd in the smaller, more intimate gym, where, unlike most football stadiums, there is no chance of being rained on during the halftime performance. Still other dancers prefer competition season because they find the excitement of competing against other dance teams for local, regional, or national titles invigorating.

Spring show, the final performance of the year, is the favorite event for many dancers. To them, few things rival dancing in the spotlight, knowing that their families and friends are in the audience watching. Then there are those dancers whose favorite season is the one they are currently in. They simply love the thrill of the performance anywhere, anytime.

The roar of an enthusiastic crowd is amplified by the walls of a gym or stadium. For dancers, this can be invigorating as they rush onto the floor to perform during a basketball game.

Competition

Dance team differs from other competitive school activities. While music and sports are regulated by state or national organizations, in most areas, dance does not fall under such agencies. Instead, there are several privately owned companies that offer competitions across the United States. The National Council of Drill Team Camps (NCDTC) is comprised of several of the most prestigious companies within the dance team industry. They are all members of Dance/Drill Team

Directors of America and Texas Dance/Drill Team Educators, as well as over twelve other state associations. The companies making up NCDTC include American Dance/Drill Team, Just for Kix, Marching Auxiliaries (M.A.) Dance, ShowMakers of America, ShowTime International, and Starmakers Dance and Performance Camps. NCDTC helps unify contest rules and regulations and entry divisions to bring more uniformity to the dance team industry.

The director of each team determines what competitions his or her team will attend each year. Some directors choose to attend only one, while others may select several. A director may have a loyalty to one company, or he or she may elect to attend several competitions with different companies. The companies offer competitions at the regional, state, national, and even the international levels. At each level, there are divisions for every age group and team size.

For dance team performers and the audiences they entertain, the many different styles of dance add variety to the art form. The following descriptions are used by the American Dance and Drill Team School in their contest entry process. Though there are many other forms of dance, these are the styles most commonly used by dance teams.

Jazz focuses on the technical aspect of traditional studio jazz, incorporating leaps, turns, and technical moves. Props or pom pons are not used. The music for jazz routines varies and might be from a Broadway show, a classic rock favorite, or even a Top 40 hit. In addition to the music, the age and ability level of the performers will dictate the elements included in the jazz routine.

Kick includes varied kick sequences performed with proper kick technique. Kicks must be performed to at least 60 percent of the music. The high kick routine has been a crowd pleaser since the dawn of the Kilgore College Rangerettes, and their unique style has often been copied but never equaled. With their annual performance in the Macy's Thanksgiving Day Parade, the famous Radio City Music Hall Rockettes have set the standard for the precision kick line with their perfectly synchronized kick routines. Other than the game itself, nothing seems to bring a football crowd to its feet more than a group of young ladies, stretched across the field, hooked up arm over arm, kicking in complete unison as the band plays a high-energy song.

Prop routines involve using props that may be handheld or used as staging for the dance. The prop should be the main visual focus for the routine and should be used during 80 percent of the routine. Often, props may be used in conjunction with other types of dance. Props are popular during dance team competition season, especially for teams with young dancers. Whether the prop is an oversized drum, a replica of an airplane, a miniature car, a staircase, or just a handheld item, it can be painted in bright colors and even glittered, adding a wonderful

The creativity found in costuming and choreography during competition season is endless. Whether competing at the regional, state, or national level, each team strives to be unique in the hope of catching the eye of every judge.

Radio City Rockettes

Since performing on opening night on December 27, 1932, the Radio City Music Hall's Rockettes have been synonymous with that famous venue in New York City. Few people realize that this dazzling precision dance line did not originate in New York. The Rockettes made their debut in St. Louis, Missouri. In 1925, Russell Markert's first talented kick line was known as the Missouri Rockets. After seeing the Ziegfeld Follies in 1922, he knew he could have a successful dance line if he could find tall women with long legs who could tap dance and kick to eye level.

The Missouri Rockets were brought to New York by S. L. (Roxy) Rothafel, who called them the Roxyettes. The group of sixteen women has increased through the years to the current thirty-six dancers now known as the Rockettes. Their early Radio City Music Hall performances consisted of extravagant and elegantly costumed dance numbers to accompany the movies shown at the theater. Even in the 1930s, the Rockettes danced so precisely together and looked so identical that they almost seemed to move as one dancer. Today, the rigid height requirements are maintained, and each dancer must be between 5'6" and 5'10 ½". Markert always placed the shortest dancers on the ends and the tallest dancers in the middle, creating an illusion of completely uniform height.

Without a doubt, the most well-known performance for the Rockettes each year is the Radio City Christmas Spectacular, but they also perform annually in the Macy's Thanksgiving Day Parade and at the NBC Rockefeller Center Tree Lighting Ceremony. Young girls everywhere aspire to grow up to be tall enough, talented enough, and glamorous enough to be a Rockette. The thirty-six ladies are still most famous for their precision eye-level kick and tap routines, but new choreography and more creative costuming are added each year, ensuring that the legacy of Russell Markert will be everlasting.

visual to the routine. The dancers performing with props seem to enjoy using their imaginations as they get into their roles. At every competition, the props seem to become more creative and outrageous than before, with the possibilities limited only by the ingenuity of the choreographer and the budget of the team.

Pom-pon routines should consist of visual formations and strong visual effects using poms and proper dance technique. The poms should be used for 80 percent of the routine. In the past, the poms traditionally were in the school colors. However, it has become popular to use brightly colored or even neon poms to enhance the music and lively movement of the choreography. There are dance teams who use poms for every routine, and some schools have more than one performance team. There may be a dance team that performs the traditional kick or jazz routines during halftime and a pom squad that also performs at halftime, but always with poms in their hands.

A novelty routine involves dancing as a character or interpreting the theme of a song. Character costuming, props, and staging may aid in this interpretation. Novelty routines appeal to the performers who really enjoy theatrics and drama.

Military routines contain sharp arm, leg, and head movements, while utilizing visual formations and military pivots and flanks. The challenge with a military routine is making every move extremely sharp and precise. A team must spend countless hours matching every arm angle, every leg level, and every head snap. The music for a good military routine must have a strong beat.

Colorful and innovative props often enhance dance team performances. The props range in size from small handheld items to huge, life-size props that the dancers may stand on as they dance.

Hip-hop or funk routines consist of contemporary upbeat moves that are sharp and dynamic. "Street style" dance is another name for hip-hop. This style is performed to high-energy, fast-paced music with a driving beat. Hip-hop has huge appeal for young audiences. Often the routines contain elements of street dance recognized by students in an audience who are not dancers themselves. This seems to help them relate to the performers and gives them a sense of belonging. Costuming for hip-hop resembles the trendy fashions of today, also

While a team may enter several different routine categories at competition, hip-hop or funk remains a favorite among the young performers as they have more freedom of style and technique.

attracting the interest of the young nondancers in the audience.

Lyrical dance incorporates movements from classical ballet as well as modern dance and jazz. The choreography should be an interpretation of the music and lyrics, incorporating complex steps such as leaps and turns, and it should have seamless transitions from step to step, creating phrasing that matches the music. Together, the music and dancer should create one composition with a unified message. A strong lyrical dancer can really connect with the members of the audience and move them to tears if he or she can get into the emotional aspect of the music and interpret it through movement. When a team performs a lyrical routine, each dancer should understand the meaning of the lyrics and the music, and

With the graceful, smooth-flowing quality of lyrical dance, if the dancer can feel the emotion in the music and communicate that to an audience through movement, the experience can be very rewarding for both.

they should make the audience feel the emotion as well. Young dancers often have difficulty with this mature approach to movement, thus lyrical dance is more popular among high school teams.

Modern dance is a dance form that utilizes a movement vocabulary that is not from a codified syllabus such as ballet or jazz. The choreographer has the freedom to create abstract movements, shapes, and patterns to form the dance. Like lyrical dance, modern dance is more common among high school teams because the younger performers find it difficult to grasp these abstract concepts. The complex elements require a more mature dancer.

Open is a routine category that may contain a combination of styles ranging from tap to production. In a production number, a team interprets a theme through dance. The theme may be an excerpt from a Broadway show, the lyrics of a song, or an original story. The open category at competition is ideal for a team with performers who excel in different styles of dance, since a combination of dance styles can be used in this category. Not only does this have great audience appeal, but the strong jazz dancers can perform in that section, the good kickers can kick, and another group might even perform a lively pom routine. The open category definitely offers something for everyone.

Coed is a routine incorporating male and female performers. Although dance team is still largely a female-oriented activity in schools, some teams have a few boys, and there are even all-male teams. (In competition, all-male teams are often placed in the coed category.) The great thing about a coed team is the opportunity for dancers to perform partner steps,

Once a novelty at dance team competitions, coed teams are becoming more common. Not only do several teams offer performance opportunities for boys and girls in combined dances, there are some all-male teams that compete on their own.

including lifts ranging from simple to complex. Dance is certainly not a female-only art form, but it has taken longer for public schools to recognize the advantages of allowing boys to participate on dance teams. The athletic nature of dance has begun to appeal to more and more boys.

This large array of dance styles allows each dance team to focus on its strengths. Students who desire to make a team excelling in high kicks must prepare well ahead of time to gain the flexibility necessary to execute this technical move. Jazz and lyrical teams require early dance studio training from their performers. The beginning dancer may adapt sooner to pom, prop, and novelty routines. Of course, the popularity of music videos has definitely increased the interest in hip-hop/funk for all ages and ability levels.

When entering competition, each team must enter the division appropriate to the age of its members and the size of the team. American Dance and Drill Team School classifies the divisions as follows: Mascots (prekindergarten through kindergarten), Elementary (first through third grades), Intermediate (fourth through sixth grades), Junior Private (seventh through ninth grades), Junior High/Middle School (sixth through ninth grades), Senior Private (high school age through twenty years old), and College (active college dance teams).

High school teams are classified according to the number of members on the team. The team sizes are as follows: small (one to fifteen members), medium (sixteen to twenty-nine members), large (thirty to forty-nine members), and super (fifty or more members).

The awards vary from company to company. The major dance and drill team companies have their contest rules, regulations, and entry information available on their Web sites.

Each team is unique and has its own style. There are many types of dance that can be performed, and each team will develop strength in different ones. While one team may excel in jazz, another may be stronger in high kick, and yet another in hip-hop. Most teams will dance in several different categories, working to develop skills in each one. Teams that compete in championships will have to enter several different categories of dance, requiring them to work to improve in different areas.

When preparing for a performance, not only must attention to detail be given to each and every dance move, but costuming and makeup require careful consideration as well. The application of makeup may enhance the theme of a performance.

Dress, Costuming, and Makeup

While some teams have a traditional uniform that changes very little over the years, others change their uniforms every few years or even yearly. Different performance venues offer different costuming opportunities.

The Kilgore Rangerette uniform is still the red top, blue skirt, white leather belt, white leather gauntlets, trademark white hat, and boots that Gussie Nell Davis designed back in 1940. The only noticeable change in that uniform has been the shortening of the skirt over the years.

Many high school teams have traditional uniforms closely mirroring the Rangerette uniform with variations on the hat. However, unlike the Rangerette uniform, sequined artwork is an important element to the design. While this type of field uniform is great for the traditional halftime routines, it does not work as well for those teams performing flashy jazz, pom, or even an occasional hip-hop routine on the football field. In recent years, it has become popular for a team to have multiple costumes to coordinate with the style of dance they perform each week. Colorful costuming adds to the visual effect of every dance.

Even for those teams having a traditional uniform for football season, competition season and spring show usually bring opportunities for creative and flashy costuming. When a team packs for competitions, the director usually prepares a packing list to insure that each dancer arrives with every costume and accessory for the dances she is in. Although there is not a category for best costuming, no team wants to be outdone by another. Sequins and rhinestones are added to every inch of costumes, even the shoes!

The performance makeup has become just as flashy as the costumes themselves. Once, theatrical makeup was all that was necessary. A little blue eye shadow, some eye liner, mascara, blush, powder, and lipstick were the staples in a dance team member's makeup bag, but not any-more. Some teams even wear makeup colors that coordinate with their costumes.

Often, prospective dance team members inquire about the need for wearing makeup. The new dancers may have never applied makeup to their faces, but they must learn that this is an important aspect of performance.

CHAPTER 5

Benefits of Dance Team

Dance team is an art form that requires dedication and determination from its participants. As the teammates work countless hours toward a common goal, they are learning discipline that will benefit them for their entire lives. Working with others is a skill necessary to be successful in life. As they are guided by their directors, students learn to respect and accept authority.

Among the possible careers in the dance industry, performing as a professional dancer is one many young students dream of. Competitions hosted by professional dance teams like the Dallas Cowboys Cheerleaders may lead a dancer on the path toward such a career.

Dancing also provides an enjoyable form of exercise that can become a lifelong activity. Today, many young people live sedentary lifestyles as they sit in front of the television or computer. Dance team members must stay physically fit to keep up with the demands of their art. The rigorous rehearsals provide the perfect workout sessions.

Many lifelong friendships begin on dance teams. Many high school dancers stay in touch with their fellow team members. After spending four years rehearsing, performing, and traveling together on their dance team, they have developed a bond that they may likely never lose. A close team will develop almost a family type of relationship.

Finally, one of the most valuable benefits of being on a dance team is learning responsibility. Team members are easily able to transfer the discipline required in dance team to other areas of their lives, including their studies and, later, careers.

There are several careers relating to dance, depending on the path a student wants to follow. They include teaching, choreography, performance, and marketing. Sometimes, one opportunity may even lead to another.

Many former dance team members go on to become dance team instructors, sometimes at their high school. Others continue to dance in professional dance teams, such as the Dallas Cowboys Cheerleaders, or join ballet and other dance companies that perform all over the world.

Even for students who will never participate in a dance performance after dance team, their experiences will most likely benefit them in their career. The organizational skills, interpersonal skills, responsibility, determination, dedication, and sense of pride in a job well done will certainly have an influence on their work ethic for the rest of their lives. Dance team has a lasting influence on every girl and boy who is fortunate enough to have been a part of such a worthwhile activity.

Kicking into the Future

When Gussie Nell Davis's Rangerettes performed back in 1940, she did not know that the popularity of dance teams would transform the activity into the competitive entertainment industry that it is today. The

As dance team performances continue to progress from football fields and competitions into the professional world, the popularity of the art will grow. The opportunities abound for dancers of all ages.

opportunities continue to abound for both males and females of many ages. No longer a fall activity limited to the football field, the sport of dance team flourishes all year in gymnasiums, on stages, and virtually anywhere there is room to dance. The boundaries are infinite, limited only by the creativity of the directors, choreographers, and the dancers themselves.

As sports teams prevail, so will the demand for dancers. The community peewee teams aspire to be like pro teams in many ways, including having their very own cheerleaders on the sidelines. This opens doors for more tiny dancers to make their debut. All of these future dancers must take lessons to prepare for their upcoming auditions, leading to an increased demand for dance studios. Many of these studios will create their own dance teams to enter in competitions all over the country.

Each year at competitions, the performers seem to get younger and younger. Moreover, there has been a steady increase in the number of young men involved. As the talent continues to grow at all age levels, more dancers want to be a part of the excitement. Dance team will continue to prosper in the years to come as today's dancers grow up to train the next dance team generation. Gussie Nell Davis's legacy just keeps on kicking.

Glossary

audition To try out for something; to be judged.

choreographer A person who makes up dance steps.

choreography The steps of a dance.

color guard A team spirit activity that involves a spectacular display of flags and other props, most notably mock rifles and sabers.

director The instructor or teacher for the team; the person in charge.

endurance The ability to sustain a prolonged stressful activity.

extracurricular Activity falling outside the regular school day, such as athletics and dance.

goal A desired outcome.

hopeful Someone who hopes to make the team; someone trying out for the team.

legendary Well known; famous.

lyrical Having a smooth flowing quality; emotionally expressive.

majorette A baton twirler.

pageantry The collection of team spirit activities that includes dance teams, marching bands, and cheerleading, among others; a spectacular performing arts presentation.

phrase A short sequence of dance moves.

portfolio A set of pictures, articles, and other documents that is presented to show one's accomplishments.

precision Exactness.

prop An article that is carried or used by a performer during a performance, such as a dance.

routine An orchestrated performance that is often repeated during a performing season.

sacrifice Something that is given up in pursuing a goal; the act of foregoing something in pursuit of the goal.

sedentary Inactive.

showmanship A knack for performing.

sideline The space immediately outside the lines along either side of a football or other sports field.

spring show The recital or concert given by a dance team in the spring.

squad A small group engaged in a common effort.

technique The manner in which the physical movements are executed by a dancer; generally, a way of doing things.

tryout An audition.

For More Information

American Dance and Drill Team
P.O. Box 1189
Salado, TX 76571
(800) 462-5719
e-mail: danceadts@aol.com
Web site: http://www.danceadts.com

Dance Spirit
Lifestyle Media, Inc.
110 William Street, 23rd Floor
New York, NY 10038
(646) 459-4800
Web site: http://www.dancespirit.com

Marching Auxiliaries/M.A. Dance
P.O. Box 940605
Plano, TX 75094
(800) 977-7933
Web site: http://www.madance.com/home.htm

Showmakers of America
P.O. Box 1789
San Marcos, Texas 78667-1789

(800) 522-8010

Web site: http://www.showmakerscamps.com

Showtime International, Inc.

P.O. Box 4200

Lago Vista, TX 78645

(800) 776-5425

Web site: http://www.showtimeint.com

Starmakers Dance and Performance Camps

508 Lookout Drive, Suite 14 #99

Richardson, TX 75080

(800) 521-9716

Web site: http://www.starmakersdance.com

Web Sites

Due to the changing nature of Internet links, the Rosen Publishing Group, Inc., has developed an online list of Web sites related to the subject of this book. This site is updated regularly. Please use this link to access the list:

http://www.rosenlinks.com/team/dance

For Further Reading

Allan, J., M. D. Ryan, and Robert E. Stephens. *The Healthy Dancer: Dance Medicine for Dancers.* Princeton, NJ: Princeton Book Company, 1987.

Franklin, Eric. *Conditioning for Dance.* Champaign, IL: Human Kinetics, 2003.

Horosko, Marian, and Judity R. F. Kupersmith. *The Dancer's Survival Manual: Everything You Need to Know About Being a Dancer . . . Except How to Dance.* New York, NY: Harper & Row Publishers, 1987.

Howse, Justin, and Moira McCormack. *Dance Technique and Injury Prevention.* London, England: A & C Black, 2000.

Porterfield, Jason. *Band Front: Color Guard, Drum Majors, and Majorettes* (Team Spirit!). New York, NY: Rosen Publishing Group, 2007.

Sawyer, Gina. *American Dance Team Leader: #1 Guide for Dance Captains, Officers, and Leaders.* Gina Sawyer, 2004.

Singer, Lynn. *Cheerleading* (Team Spirit!). New York, NY: Rosen Publishing Group, 2007.

Valliant, Doris. *Dance Teams* (Let's Go Team: Cheer, Dance, March). Broomall, PA: Mason Crest Publishers, 2003.

Bibliography

DallasCowboys.com. "Dallas Cowboys Cheerleaders: History."
Retrieved October 2, 2005 (http://www.dallascowboys.com/
cheerleaders/history.cfm).

National Council of Drill Team Camps. "Welcome to the NCDTC . . .
The Authority in Dance Teams." Retrieved October 1, 2005
(http://www.danceadts.com/ncdtc).

Pennington, Joyce. "History of Dance/Drill Team . . . The First Twenty
Years." Retrieved October 1, 2005 (http://www.danceadts.com/
edsupport/history_drillteam.htm).

RadioCity.com. "Radio City Rockettes: History." Retrieved January 29,
2006 (http://www.radiocity.com/eventcalendar/home#).

Rangerette.com. "Meet the Rangerettes: History." Retrieved October 1,
2005 (http://www.rangerette.com/history.asp).

Index

About the Author

Mary Kaye Coachman has been the director of the Ellison High School Emeralds for twenty-six years. During that time, the Emeralds have won several national championships at the American Dance and Drill Team national competition. Coachman has received three Outstanding Director awards from A & M Dance Classic and American Dance/Drill Team Nationals in the last three years. She currently teaches teen leadership, dance, and drill team at Ellison High School in Killeen, Texas. Coachman is also a staff member of American Dance and Drill Team School. She enjoys choreographing for a local theater group in her spare time. A graduate of the University of Mary Hardin-Baylor, she did postgraduate work at Southwest Texas State University to earn her Texas teacher certification in dance. Coachman began dancing at the age of ten and always knew she would somehow make it her career.

Series Consultant: Susan Epstein

Photo Credits

Cover, p. 31 Rowlett High School Bootbackers Historian Committee; title page, pp. 5, 19, 34 Cheerleaders of America; pp. 7, 26 Frank Coachman; pp. 8, 25, 44, 47, 51, 52 MA Dance; pp. 9, 10, 11 Kilgore Rangerettes; p. 14 © S. Carmona/ Corbis; pp.16, 17, 22 Eastern Washington Elite Dance; pp. 21, 33, 36 NBAE/ Getty Images; pp. 27, 45 Simone Associates, Lebanon, Pennsylvania; p. 29 Eastern Dance Association; p. 38 Champion Tours & Events, Orlando, Florida; p. 41 © Reuters/Corbis; p. 43 © Karen Kasmauski/Corbis; p. 49 Plano Dance Force Team; p. 54 Champion Dance Nationals, Orlando, Florida.

Designer: Gene Mollica; Editor: Wayne Anderson; Photo Researcher: Marty Levick